BUILDING RELATIONSHIPS
Get the Best from People

Uwem Essia

All rights reserved. No part of this book may be reproduced, distributed, or transmitted in any form or by any means, including photocopying, recording or other electronic or mechanical methods, without the prior written permission of the publisher, except in the case of brief quotations embodied in critical reviews and certain other noncommercial uses permitted by copyright law.

Copyright © June 8 2022, Uwem Essia. All rights reserved.

ABOUT THE AUTHOR

Prof. Uwem Essia obtained a Ph.D. degree in Economics from the University of Calabar, Nigeria in 2003. He has worked in several Nigerian Universities and in Cameroon. He is a researcher, trainer, consultant, and motivational speaker, and has authored (co-authored) several books on research methodology, political economy, security and peacebuilding, spirituality and mindfulness, international affairs, and development, among other areas.

ABOUT THE AUTHOR

INTRODUCTION

CHAPTER ONE: FUNDAMENTALS OF RELATIONSHIP BUILDING

    Why Build and Sustain Relationships?

    Basis for Relationships

    Kinds of Relationships

    You are at the Center of the Universe

    Relationship Building is a Continuing Process

    Relationships and Trust-Building

CHAPTER TWO: ESTABLISH RELATIONSHIPS BEFORE YOU NEED THEM

    Establishing Relationships in a Crisis

    Managing Cultural Diversity and Friendship

CHAPTER THREE: BUILDING RELATIONSHIPS WITH PEOPLE WHO HOLD POSITIONS OF AUTHORITY

    Sustaining Relationships

CHAPTER FOUR: MENDING BROKEN RELATIONSHIPS

CHAPTER FIVE: RELATIONSHIPS WITH ADVERSARIES (DINNING WITH THE DEVIL)

CHAPTER SIX: LIVING AN ORGANIZED LIFE AS KEY TO HEALTHY RELATIONSHIPS

CHAPTER SEVEN: RELATIONSHIP BUILDING AND LEADERSHIP

CONCLUDING REMARKS

SOURCES

INTRODUCTION

The book *BUILDING RELATIONSHIPS: Get the Best from People* identifies qualitative relationships as a capital asset and motivational currency needed by everyone who seeks to get the best from others. Relationships determine what people are willing to sacrifice to support your dreams and aspirations.

Political leaders who nurture and sustain qualitative relationships long before elections are most likely to enjoy 'cult' followership. Similarly, leaders of corporate organizations will get the best from their line managers and other employees if they are perceived as good relationship builders.

Marriages, business partnerships, associations, and friendships become stable, self-sustaining, and mutually beneficial to the parties when they are deliberately nurtured, managed, and supported to grow.

The book explains how to build relationships under different conditions, why many relationships fail, and provides tips for nurturing and sustaining qualitative relationships. This book is intended for everyone because we all need relationships.

CHAPTER ONE: FUNDAMENTALS OF RELATIONSHIP BUILDING

Relationships are the building blocks of our personal lives and human organization at all levels. Success in any field or activity requires having good relationships. We need friends, partners, co-workers, neighbors, relatives, and even adversaries. Isolationism is not sustainable, as it is often said, 'no man is an island.' Our relationships added up is the foundation of a thriving society. We need people to contribute their ideas, take a stand with, and get the work done

As individuals, we motivate others and they motivate us as well. It is a necessary human value to relate to and care for others. The health, happiness, and overall wellbeing of our children, neighbors, colleagues, and partners are valuable to us, and in many cases we go out of our way to ensure that they are fine. We often do so alongside pushing ourselves to overcome obstacles and take on challenges in our personal lives. It is important that we take our problems seriously. But no matter how we try by ourselves, our optimal productivity still depends on the relationships that we have with others. Qualitative relationships will always help us to do much better as individuals, employees, employers, and leaders.

Relationships do not just happen; they need to be cultivated, nurtured, and grown. Relationship building requires enormous personal and social skills. But at the foundation of it is that we need to be charming, witty, receptive, and sensitive to the needs of others.

Why Build and Sustain Relationships?

Relationships are necessary because we are social beings. We exist and experience life within, but the act of living is manifested outside us as we relate to other human beings and the rest of creation. You need people to live out your life, and without others life is not expressed. The purpose of our lives as individuals has to be expressed in relation to other persons.

Suppose you want to create a viable non-governmental organization (NGO). People have to help you create it, and ultimately participate in its activities. You need to relate with various parties to realize the NGO. So an inescapable question to ask has to be, 'what kind of relationships do you need to make it happen'? A simplified process for creating the NGO and the relationships involved are explained below.

1. Get people to help you register the NGO and mobilize people to join?

Even if you can, it is tedious to do all the planning and legwork by yourself. Getting others around makes it easier and fun-filled.

2. Secure local approval and cooperation.

To register the NGO you have to file the papers to seek and obtain approvals. Having some friends in the relevant government circles might help you work the bureaucratic hoops out easily. You may need to build new relationships if none existed.

3. Have offices and meeting hall/space

You may need an agent to help you rent offices and meeting halls. However, a friend may decide to provide you with temporary offices and halls without much cost. Another friend may offer free entertainment during the early-stage meetings. In many ways, having relationships increases functioning and makes a complex assignment a lot easier.

4. Identifying and Enlisting the NGO members/participants

Your old friends, neighbors, co-workers, relatives, and so on may the larger part of your early stage membership, and help you to enlist others. You need as many members/participants, officials/facilitators, and patrons/sponsors as possible. The more relationships the merrier. You also need patrons and funders. It is important that you get the right people and have them cooperate with you. You must have a way to get them to attend meetings, pay their dues, and participate in other activities towards development of the NGO. Overall, the more people you know, the easier it will be to organize an NGO and the more useful the NGO will be.

Basis for Relationships

At its core, a relationship is built on a one-to-one basis. For our NGO example, it can be said rightly that people support a cause that they believe will add value to themselves and the larger society. Yet it can be said that people are more interested or willing to be involved in a group when those they have relationships with are already involved.

We need relationships in order to win more supporters/allies to our side. In this case, the NGO will grow when those who know and trust us set out to enlist others. This is why it is important to have around us people who love and trust us. Hence, the quality and quantity of our relationships give meaning and richness to our work and lives. We all need a community of people to share the joys and the struggles of organizing our lives and achieving success. Otherwise, life loses its meaning and material and emotional relevance. When you have done well and people praise you for doing so, and when you fail people say you can do better next time. It is relationships that give life meaning.

Kinds of Relationships

Relationships are of different kinds but they all matter. They can be initiated in different patterns. It may just start with a smile, or saying hello to someone. For instance, being nice to a groceries shop seller may qualify you to benefit from some credit terms and or a discount. The shop owner will most likely remember your smiles and attractive manners and give you wholesale prices although you bought as a retailer. The relationship with the groceries seller is quite different from that with your neighbor, medical doctor, lawyer, or office colleague.

The more relationships you have with people, the better. You never know when they will come in handy. For example, a town crier may be the person you need to help you pass the information on your products to others. So do not minimize any relationship. You need as many friends and well-wishers as possible. Building friendships will pay off in ways you may never have anticipated.

You are at the Center of the Universe

Each individual is like a hub, pivot, or spindle of a wheel and each spoke represents a relationship with another person. It takes a lot of spokes to hold the wheel together. The wheel is the external system that holds various relationships into a system connecting us to the rest of the world. The universe has enough space to accommodate as many wheels and spokes as possible. Relationships take time to be set up and are sustained by continuing interactions and exchanges. If you wait for others to establish relationships with you first, you may spend a lot of time waiting.

The benefits of relationships have to be mutual. You can't have a good relationship when you are either a lone giver or receiver. It doesn't work that way. The benefits and costs have to be distributed mutually for the relationship to have sustainability. The longevity of a relationship is founded on the reciprocity of those involved. Otherwise one party feels used or abused and will sooner or later withdraw. Sincerity and commitment to others are the foundation of a sound relationship. Sustainable or enduring relationships are formed when parties genuinely like and or need each other, we have what others need and wish to exchange it for what we need.

Relationship Building is a Continuing Process

Building relationships has to be a lifelong process. A few moments for exchanging pleasantries may just be sufficient. Relationships are nurtured over time. Maintaining relationships with many persons is possible and necessary. Human resources are the most critical for personal wellbeing and productivity. Although pressures of life and the associated risks of relating with people may make us think or act otherwise. But it doesn't change the fact that relationship building is the most important thing to do. Getting to know how to make productive use of relationships is of critical importance to our success because in many ways relationships are the key to solving a problem or getting the job done. Building and sustaining strong relationships is central to our work and life.

Relationships can be described as a foundation that has to be laid for other developments to take place. The bigger the project, the more relationships are needed. For example, if you are a mediator set to reconcile warring factions within a large community, you have to get to know people on the rival sides well before trying to get them together for a negotiated settlement. It is easier to persuade people you are close to than total strangers. However, relationship building is an expensive business that requires the commitment of valuable resources, especially time and money. You must commit time to attend to the affairs of those you seek to have relationship with.

Relationships and Trust-Building

Relationship building is about trust-building. We need to make others trust us. People are willing to work and share their lives with those they trust. When trust is missing, collaborating is inhibited. Worrying about the risk of losing out increases when trust is in short supply. Disagreements erupt frequently over flimsy issues. Like salt in a soup, mutual trust gives relationships its taste. Trust assures you of good return to your investment in relationship building. People are often more willing to commit resources to projects where the partners share their interests and aspirations.

Consider again our NGO creation example. Establishing an NGO involves several communities of stakeholders. You need to enlist the support and participation of various groups of persons. The engagement has to start on a small scale and extend progressively to a wider sphere. A weekly or monthly (physical) meeting for the officials may do. A chat group of all members can help galvanize the views of all the members. It may be necessary to plan events regularly For example, you can jointly sponsor an evening of cultural sharing. If the evening is successful, you will have gained some shared trust and confidence on which to build future interactions. You can plan several similar events that will build trust over a period of time. The more meetings held the more the gains, and the faster the factors inhibiting interactions are identified and dealt with.

CHAPTER TWO: ESTABLISH RELATIONSHIPS BEFORE YOU NEED THEM

Make building relationships a way of life because qualitative relationships are never too much. You don't have to need them immediately. Build relationships with nearly everyone, but make the qualitative relationships more intimate. Do not ignore the *bad guys* because you may need them sometimes. For example, if you already have a good relationship with the 'area boys,' they may spare you while rioting. And you may be in a good position to resolve a conflict between them and other groups say, farmers in your community. It is much the same as your jurist friends can help to vet and sign your agreements at no cost.

Establishing Relationships in a Crisis

Crises may offer a good opportunity to build relationships. While it may seem unusual, make the most of your crisis or an acquaintance's crisis. Participating in finding solutions to your organization's or a friend's problems makes it difficult for you to be forgotten. Do not hesitate to help when and where you can, it is the easiest way to attract positive attention. You can also build relationships when you are in need as well because those who are ready to help when you are in trouble easily become your true friends.

Here are some tips for building relationships in crisis.

a. Focus on the key individuals and be deliberate - during a crisis, many individuals come your way. Focus on the key person and get their contacts. Exchange greetings thereafter and request to add them to your chat groups. Get to know them better. Those who appreciate you will respond positively. Others may hesitate. Harvest the interested individuals and move on. Where possible, face-to-face meetings may grow intimacy faster

b. Connect to people with friendliness - those who are able to make friends connect to people faster. Friendly smile and kind words in times of crisis connect you to people faster. We all have things in common and building friendship makes finding them easier.

c. Ask people questions - people in trouble find comfort in talking about their predicament, and what they think. Listen to them with rapt attention. It makes them feel that you care. It is not a time to judge or find fault in them. If you ask people about themselves and then take the time to listen attentively, they can become your best friends.

d. Tell people about yourself – when people tell you about their situation, reciprocate by sharing with them the aspects of your life that resound with their story. It makes them perceive that you trust them and they should be able to trust you. Tell them what you genuinely care about and what you think.

e. Go places and do things - it is easier to have more friends when you meet more people and show readiness to relate with them. So attend picnics, conferences, events, fundraisers, parties, playgrounds, bowling alleys, little league games, bake sales, and so on and make more friends.

f. *Accept people the way they are* – accepting that we are different will help you connect readily with different people while having a good understanding of their strengths and vulnerabilities. We are different in several ways. Friendship is built faster when we understand that disagreeing on diverse issues is normal and that no one likes being judged. Also, it is useful to assume that other people want to form relationships, too. Underneath the grouchiest looking person is often a lonely person seeking to be touch with love and attention.

g. *Overcome your fear of rejection* – kill the fear that you will be rejected by trying. Tell yourself that 'yes' and 'no' are the possible answers that an individual you approach for a discussion may give. A 'no' answer means you have to approach more people. Be at home with the fact that you will be rejected sometimes.

h. *Be persistent* - people are often shy and suspicious when meeting others for the first time. Help to break the ice by opening up first. It may take a while to win trust. If you consider that the individual will make a qualitative friend, then be committed to making him or her one. The chances that you'll succeed if you press on are high.

i. Create spaces for people to be involved in your affairs – many people would participate in responsible discussion/learning chat groups and blogs if invited. This can get more persons to participate in your affairs. If you genuinely enjoy associating with people, many of them will be willing to get closer to you where the spaces exist.

Managing Cultural Diversity and Friendship

The tips for managing cultural diversity for friendship are the following:

a. Learn about the person's culture.

Make effort to understand the cultures of your regular and prospective friends. It will make you appreciate and tolerate them more. Any little effort will go a long way in showing that you care enough to find out about their values and how their views are shaped. Cultures are neither good nor bad. Read about different cultures because it will enhance your ability to relate with others. Take yourself mentally to the center of your friends' cultures and you will understand them more.

Also, while dealing with people of minority groups especially, be mindful of what makes them different and respect their sensitivities and boundaries. Adjusting yourself to accept the culturing of others, even where uncomfortable, is healthy for relationship building. If you are willing to take risks and put yourself in a situation in which you might feel uncomfortable, for the sake of making others happy people will be more inclined to want to get to know you.

It follows that you don't minimize the pains of others or emphasize their mistakes or the perceived weaknesses of their cultures. Stand with them when they feel oppressed or are in trouble. Take actions in support of a legitimate cause. People appreciate you more when they feel that you are standing by them while they are experiencing crisis. Strong relationships are forged when people act courageously on behalf of each other.

b. Treat the shortcomings of others as mistakes

Accept that we all make mistakes, and consider ignorance the basis for most mistakes that human beings make. We certainly do better when we know better. Do not readily judge others. Take it that we are all learning beings. Every mistake is a learning opportunity for those who make them, and those watching them. So it is simply how we perceive it.

Note that it is in the nature of man to be forgiving. So learn to forgive people even before they are able to apologize and you will retain so many friends. You make mistakes and expect to be forgiven, so forgive others, especially when you observe that they have the right intentions.

The saying, 'do to others what you want done to you' is common to nearly all religions and moral philosophies. Being mindful of this maxim will make us live well with people and build productive relationships. At whatever level you are in the society, sharing your life with others will make you more successful and happier. But it requires an ability to let go of the mistakes that others make and be tolerant the way you would wish to be tolerated and forgiven.

c. Start from the people around you

We all have relationships. There is hardly a person without acquaintances, relatives, colleagues, neighbors and friends. Invest a little more on strengthening the ties with them. Communicate more and be more concerned about their issues. Greet them with a smile and genuinely ask how they are. Doing these will make you feel better and make your relationships more fulfilling.

Nowadays growing uncertainties, especially the risk of being scammed, kidnapped or harmed in other ways make people become excessively cautious about relationships. The restrictive mandates associated with the COVID pandemic equally limits the desire for face-to-face interactions. All the same, it is still important to brace up and take all necessary steps to relate with others.

Make concerted efforts to meet people physically and via online platforms. Join clubs, associations, and media platforms where the people you would love to relate to are found and take steps to enhance your visibility. You are likely to meet more people if you determine to do so.

CHAPTER THREE: BUILDING RELATIONSHIPS WITH PEOPLE WHO HOLD POSITIONS OF AUTHORITY

Persons in leadership positions may be more difficult to relate with because they are often overwhelmed by work, and several person seek their attention for favors. Here are some tips to help you build relationship with people in authority; elected officials, business leaders, and heads of large organizations, and so on.

a. Don't be intimidated.

People in positions of authority are human beings like you, albeit often busy. They need genuine relationships like everyone else does.

b. Listen more and speak less

Politicians in government and leaders in the corporate world often see themselves as highly intelligent persons. So except you are asked to say something, be content with listening to their stories and withhold your judgment. Except you are recognized and asked to give an expert view, remain silent. Regularly cheer them for their significant contributions. Top leaders love praises when they do well.

c. Readily give them what you have

The assumption that top political and corporate leaders do not appreciate gifts because they are already rich is unfounded. Giving is not only about money. Painted frames, wood carvings, sculptures, and so on can make them really happy. Your services and attention may equally matter. Do not under-value what you have, they are certainly what many people need. Also, making valuable and supportive comments and 'liking' on their online media posts consistently without being fanatic can improve your relationship with them.

Anything you are able to offer them as individuals outside the context of their leadership can cement your relationship with them.

Sustaining Relationships

Relationships are living realities. Like other living things, relationships need to be nurtured and kept alive. Below are tips of what has to be done to grow and sustain relationships.

a. Pay attention to people

Create time to pay attention to people. Visit them and spend some time with them where possible. If they stay far aware, then call them regularly and exchange chats. Celebrate their anniversaries – birthdays, wedding, graduation, and so on – even when they appear to forget yours. This will take some of your time, but is worth it; the time spent will make a difference by keeping you on their mind.

b. Communicate openly

Be frank and economical with words. Do not make promises that you can't fulfill. Most top political and corporate leaders will appreciate if you are able to sway public opinion in their favor. Create a page, blog, or website that connects you to the wider world and, as often as you can, make true non-judgmental comments and reviews on them.

Most top leaders are lonely people. They know that many people around them are barely present for the season. They will love to discuss with people that they believe truly care. So make yourself available. When people don't have a chance to talk about important issues, misunderstandings can occur and tensions often build up. Communication is a discipline that has to be practiced regularly; it's like food supplements and regular exercises.

c. Allow yourself to be cheated sometimes

Relationships with political and corporate leaders are not always financially gainful especially at the beginning. Quite often people holding top positions take others for granted and may not be there when you need them most. Note that you may be doing the same to those following you.

Generally, we tend to cheat those we love and love easily those we cheat. It is certainly unfair, but of course, the world has never been fair.

d. Appreciate little favors

Generally we love those who appreciate and tell others about what we do for them. So except they prefer not to be mentioned, be openly grateful for the help you are receiving from them. Appreciate the little favors and reciprocate favors you receive from people and get more. It is important also that you make good use of what you get from top leaders because they'll love to see their support have the right impact.

e. Go out of your way to do something nice

Go out of your way to do something innovative and extraordinarily different. It is normal to associate readily with successful people. Extend yourself positively. Be spectacular for something good. Go a little out of your way to do things that touch the lives of others positively and top politicians and corporate leaders will find you attractive and useful. Volunteering is an opportunity to provide quality community service. If you lend others a hand leaders are more likely to think well of you and give something back in return.

Those who make effort to do well attract others who mean well to themselves. So stretch yourself beyond what you ever imagine you could do and you will be able to build strong relationships and challenge others to partner with you for higher exploits.

Note also that loyalty to the top political and corporate leaders is very important. Even when they appear to be doing things you do not agree with now, provided it is not illegal, stay still and be ready to rise or fall with your leaders. You may not always benefit from them. Others who observed your loyalty will most likely pick you up and reward you.

CHAPTER FOUR: MENDING BROKEN RELATIONSHIPS

Like other living systems, relationships break down sometimes and needs to be mended. Best friend, blood relations, and business partners quarrel. Misunderstanding is part of the dynamics of relationships. A relationship hitting the rocks is not altogether bad. In many ways conflicts/disputes offer friends/partners the opportunity for mutual self-expression beyond pretenses and constructed niceties. The relationships that end after a few misunderstanding was not meant to be. Contrariwise, the ones that survive conflicts may get strengthened and more enduring.

Misunderstanding among people in relationships often demonstrate that the parties have deeper interests to share. A fight among two friends provides an avenue for self-examination and reflection by the parties to determine if the relationship was indeed necessary or worth it. Relationships where the parties fight more may indeed imply that they care about each other and share their greatest hopes. Below are tips to handle broken relationships.

a. Take time to listen to each other

When parties in a conflict are able to listen to themselves, then a significant aspect of the issues leading to the quarrel is being addressed. Mutual listening of parties in a conflict is a conflict resolution therapy that individuals seeking to build relationships must learn to implement. Curiously we are taught how to read, write, and speak in schools, but not how to listen. Yet listening is very important as a mark of self-discipline and a precursor for taking intentional actions.

Effective or active listening is the ability to postpone your anger and give the rival party the opportunity to state his/her side of the story. Quite often, when at least one party can patiently listen to the other, the basis for the misunderstanding may be eroded off by reasoning. Many disputes get resolved at this stage because the disputing parties are able to hear themselves and can 'respond', instead of 'react' to the situation. With reaction, emotion leads, but with responding, reasoning overwhelms emotions.

The situation is eased further where a mediator is involved. When parties in a dispute are made to listen and stay quiet while the other speaks, resolving the conflict is eased significantly. A mediator has to set the rule that each party should have his/her time to speak and should not be interrupted. One has to note what the other says and thereafter responds. As the parties speak in turn and the rival listens, reason is likely to prevail and the parties in many cases realize their mistakes.

b. Put yourself in the other person's shoes.

The next stage is when the parties have to mentally switch roles. Having heard the full story of each side, the mediator poses the question to either party, 'if you were in his/her situation what would you have done differently?' With this, the parties may readily see their fault and settle their dispute.

Quite often misunderstanding arises because people in a relationship believe in their half story and convince themselves that they are absolutely right. Once the parties are willing to examine the other side many disputes wither off.

c. Make Efforts to Correct the Situation

Problems identified in the second stage have to be addressed in the third stage. This is not be difficult because the issues behind the dispute were identified in the second stage. The parties knew where they acted wrongly. What may be required to resolve the conflict at this stage is for the parties to apologize to each other.

At least one party must be ready to act more maturely for a broken relationship to be mended on time. The more mature party is needed for the sustainability of nearly all relationships. Maturity in this case is demonstrated by readiness of the party to apply reasoning and demonstrate significant control over fleeting emotions. All human beings are egotistic in some sense, but sustainability of relationships demands that at least one party puts his/her ego under check and saves the relationship otherwise it breaks for no just cause.

The more mature party quick often understands that people may say things they don't mean while in the middle of a quarrel. With effective listening, the more mature party can wait and allow some time and space for the excessively angered party to recover so that reasoning prevails and the dispute is resolved.

Most misunderstandings that threaten relationships are due to misinformation and or ignorance. People are hardly able to say the right things when they are controlled by anger. So continue to appreciate and respect an angry friend until he/she returns the state of active listening or reasoning. This is certainly a difficult task. But it is why this book is useful and should be read by everyone.

d. Relationships can be saved when at least a party decides to act independently.

To save a relationship a party should be able and ready to act independently with a commitment to resolve the dispute. Become the more mature party and preserver of relationships because friendships are valuable assets. Make effort to unravel why the dispute exist. While doing so remain focused on what you and the other person care about most and why the relationship should be sustained despite the misunderstanding.

e. Don't give up on your principles

If at any point you discover that the relationship no longer serves your purpose, or goes against your principles, then you have to let it go. Don't give up your principles. Don't sacrifice what you believe in just to make a relationship work. If you give up on your principles, you won't be effective and the relationship won't work anyway.

But if the relationship still serves your purposes and with no possibility of the friend/partner leading you into trouble, then hang on and work out a settlement. You can take some breathing space for a while, but try not to give up on the relationship altogether. When things are the toughest, there are important lessons to be learned. It's best to keep a relationship that you consider important now or in the future than let it go on the altars of egocentrism or fleeting anger.

You can act independently to improve any relationship. Even if the other party is nt acting rightly, you can act in a way that is positive, respectful, constructive, and thoughtful. This may make you more respected and cause others to follow your lead. All said, mending broken relationships is hard but not impossible. Become the mature party and retain valuable friends. It will make them and others respect you more.

CHAPTER FIVE: RELATIONSHIPS WITH ADVERSARIES (DINNING WITH THE DEVIL)

Relationships have to be purposeful. Depending on what has to be achieved, it may be expedient to build friendships with adversaries. As it is sometimes said, 'an enemy today can become a friend tomorrow.' From disagreements at the beginning, your adversaries may become good friends or instruments for you to achieve your purpose. It does not really matter what may be happening currently because in split seconds the people who disagree with you, or are working against you today may become your allies when they understand you better. So provided your goals are well served and your adversary is not engaged in any form of criminal affairs, you can exploit available opportunities to build a sound working relationship with him/her.

But as it is often said, 'in dinning with the devil you need a long spoon'. You have to set the boundaries of the relationship as much as you can for purposes that you intend the relationship to serve. The boundaries may be shifted progressively with time either to expand or contract depending on new information that you have on the individual. Building a friendship with an adversary is easier when you have the capacity and understanding to control it.

It is not just about individuals, increasingly competing organizations are finding it expedient to collaborate to protect their common interest. For instance, competing telecom services providers may consider it needful to collaborate to set prices and provide joint infrastructure that they use commonly. The phenomenon where competing organizations collaborate has come to be known as 'coopetition'.

Similarly, warring armed groups often have to sheath their swords and agree on having a ceasefire for a period of time. They can exchange of prisoners, and provide safe passages for journalists, humanitarian aid, and health workers. Politicians of different political parties may agree to present consensus candidates for some electoral positions and pool their campaign and electioneering resources to serve that joint purpose. Building a healthy working relationship with an adversary shows that you are pursuing higher goals, and can be a key source of strength. But it has to be handled in ways that show clearly that the parties will gain mutually and the risk of undercutting by either side is minimized to the barest minimum. Third parties (mediators/negotiators) may play important roles when dealing with an adversary.

Making effort to reconcile or collaborate with adversaries is a strength. In many instances, it diffuses tensions, prevents/deescalates conflicts, and diverts resources that should have been used to service a conflict for more productive uses. The more adversaries that you are able to share common interests with the better. We all become stronger when connected to others, especially those who may pose major threats as adversaries. Your adversaries need not be converted to your friends. What is important is building cooperative systems where the risk of possible attack or sabotage from them is minimized since you share same interests no matter how small. The relationships you build today can last you over an entire lifetime, and beyond to benefit future generations. Building relationships with adversaries can be challenging because people are unique and complex and there is no easy formula.

CHAPTER SIX: LIVING AN ORGANIZED LIFE AS KEY TO HEALTHY RELATIONSHIPS

Building relationships has to be deliberate and planned, and it takes skills and being organized at all levels to achieve success. Below are tips for having your life well organized.

1. Regularly conduct a Strength, Weaknesses, Opportunities, and Threats (SWOT) Analysis of your Life

Your success or failure begins right inside of you. You have to act consciously and deliberately, and the first step is conducting a periodic Strength, Weaknesses, Opportunities, and Threats (SWOT) analysis on yourself.

- ***Strengths*** are your abilities, or capacities that you have to identify, harness, and utilize optimally for your wellbeing, and to support others and society. They include competencies, and other spiritual, physical, and emotional attributes. Your strengths can grow through ongoing learning and self-discovery.

- ***Weaknesses*** are the incapacities and vulnerabilities that restrain you from realizing your aspirations. These include a lack of necessary competencies, and a cocktail of spiritual, physical, and emotional attributes and deficiencies. Aging and sicknesses are among the weaknesses that may be difficult to reverse. The impact of some weaknesses may be minimized or wedged with new learning, change in vocation, or relocation to more enabling environments. For instance, aging may be wedged with dieting, taking up new vocations that requires less physical stress, and having a planned early retirement.

- ***Opportunities*** are the avenues, enablement, and spaces where your strengths can be put to do productive work. They are the existing/emerging spaces and platforms for transforming creativity into innovations and capacities to capabilities. It is often said that life offers opportunities always, but we need enlightenment marched with adequate motivation/incentives to optimally realize them. We need to continually train ourselves to readily identify opportunities and utilize them.

- ***Threats*** are the systems, activities, predispositions, and factors that generate doubts or fear. There are two sides to threats. On the one hand, they can compel us to initiate proactive steps that reduce our vulnerability to the associated risks occurring. That way we are able to minimize the fear element from the threat and rather turn it into an opportunity for disruptive innovational thinking. On the other, we let the fear factor consume us, by not taking the necessary preventive/preemptive steps.

An organized individual will conduct the SWOT analysis regularly to take into account the emerging dynamics and changing values. What was a strength yesterday may become a weakness now! For instance, a Ph.D. degree was certainly a strength when you secured a teaching job soon after graduation. But close to your retirement age, it can become an albatross inhibiting you from preparing adequately for an active post-retirement life.

2. Acknowledge that we go into relationships with flaws and strengths

Accept that we are all unfinished projects. Man is a spiritual being on a lifelong learning mission to add value to the universe. We should consider ourselves successful to the extent that the learning accumulated helps us to transform the universe as much as we can. The SWOT analysis will help identify your flaws and strengths. Accept that others have flaws and strengths as well. Thus in relationships, we connect to the strengths and weaknesses of individuals like us, and not ideals or theoretical constructs. Do not be carried away by your strengths or overwhelmed by your vulnerabilities. At the same time be tolerant of others because they are like you. Be content with being yourself. Keep improving what has to be improved, enduring what you can't change, and accepting others with their strengths and vulnerabilities.

As much as possible, friends/partners should mutually share information about their strengths and vulnerabilities. This will help to promote mutual understanding and minimize conflicts.

3. Have Integrity

Albeit smartness, skimming, and treachery may take you quickly to the top, but can't certainly stabilize you there long enough for you to enjoy the at-the-top experience. But integrity, hard work, and good relationships, together, may take you up at a slower pace, but in a more stable and peaceful manner that allows you to enjoy the beauty and sights of the top.

Nowadays people get enriched easily through criminal activities, like terrorism, gun-running, scamming, and trafficking in human beings and human organs, and so on. Yet integrity, hard work, and good relationships still have important roles to play in ensuring sustainable success. Those who are known to be dependable and consistent are found to be happier and consistently respected.

Ensure that your thoughts, words, and acts align. The mark of integrity is connecting your thought, acts, and words. Integrity will make people trust you easily. Integrity is thus a key pillar of relationship building and sustainability. Be honest, especially to the people around you, even when it will initially seem to hurt you or someone else. It's better for people to know that you can't do something right from the beginning than build expectations on the outcome they expect to see only to be disappointed at the end. Think well before you promise, and deliver what you promise even where it hurts.

4. Be There for Others

Relationships grow stronger and eventually become self-sustaining when the parties prioritize the mutual exchange of support. Support spans from words of encouragement, to materials and money.

5. Having the right mindset

A scientific mindset that is ready to look at the facts from all the sides is what is referred to here as the right mindset. People with the right mindset are good relationship builders because they submit more to reason than to fictions and unhelpful narratives. They are ready to put things to test. When there is failure they set out to try again. The see opportunities everywhere, and their task is to simply walk through the opportunities.

CHAPTER SEVEN: RELATIONSHIP BUILDING AND LEADERSHIP

Leadership has become quite challenging in an increasingly uncertain and crisis-prone global society. No doubt, the challenges are as well associated with an avalanche of emerging opportunities. Leaders with good capacity to build and sustain productive relationships will surely have a dependable stock of human resources to support them to success.

With globalization of the internet and air transportation, the world is getting smaller and smaller by the day. Yet diversity still exist and people are increasing divided on the basis of culture, religion, social status, and language. These divergences exist side-by-side with growing convergences occasioned by innovational revolutions. To become highly productive, today's leaders need 'melting pot' mechanisms to forge convergences among the stakeholders working with and or under them.

With the 'melting pot' mechanisms, relationship building across multiple groups of stakeholders – board members, employees, suppliers, labor unions, regulators, communities of buyers, and so on – is eased and turned to a source of power for the leaders, and a system of empowerment for the stakeholders. Empowerment of the stakeholders is mainly in terms of growing the leadership capabilities of the line managers and turning them into a pool of resources to support the self-propelling growth mission of the organization.

Some tips that the prospective leaders may use to achieve success in relationship building and growing productivity are explained below.

1. Conduct online meetings

Have regular meeting sessions with the entire group leaders to have everyone on the same page. Regular Zoom meetings can have the internal and external leaders share their perspectives on the aspect of the organization that concerns them. Such meetings allow the leader to have first-hand information on how the organization is perceived by the external stakeholders and give him/her firsthand information on how the line managers are relating to the external stakeholders. The enlarged meetings involving the external and internal parties should discuss only matters that connect the organization and its external stakeholders. Issues specific to the organization should be discussed in internal meetings with the relevant line managers and staff. Also, social media chat groups can be created for the enlarged stakeholders' group and the internal staff respectively.

2. Leaders need to update their skills regularly

The complex realities of our evolving world demands that today's managers update their skills regularly. Balancing the needs for personal development, dealing with external stakeholders and internal staff, managing the restrictive mandates imposed by the pandemic, navigating through growing insecurity and the corruptions associated with poorly monitored bureaucracies, and catching up with the fast pace of technological change are challenges that today's leaders must deal with almost on a per-second basis. Also with the trajectories of innovativeness and profitability shifting speedily, the corporate and public service leaders need to update their skills regularly.

3. *Prioritizing duties and responsibilities*

Leaders need to prioritize duties and responsibilities and create room for building relationships and resting. Today's top public and private sector leaders need to incorporate rest into their work. Dealing with the multiple challenges on daily basis can be highly exhausting. Doing so will get them more productive and still maintain their health.

There is a need to intentionally create time and space for visitations, and attending the ceremonies of loved ones. Without prioritizing and sticking to the plan, many leaders become enslaved by the work and ignore the important need to connect to people.

CONCLUDING REMARKS

The tips that you require to build and sustain productive and healthy relationships discussed above are summarized

a. Build relationships before you need them

Firstly, be confidently ready to build friendships as a deliberate process. Assume that the person you seek to relate with needs the relationship as much as you do.

Secondly, focus on building qualitative relationships with people who by your assessment can add value. In particular, people with integrity, who are hardworking, and have a reasonable sense of self-worth would most likely add value. Thirdly, make your communications clear and concise, and lastly follow up on your friendship quest.

b. Draw up a friendship prospecting map that matches your goals and aspirations

First, list the sectors, industries, and professions from where you seek to build new relationships and networks. Second, prioritize the areas set out to identify the prospective friends/collaborators. You can start from people who may need favors from you. Doing a favor to people can improve an existing relationship and or create new ones.

c. Maintain confidence

Except where it becomes necessary, keep the favors that you have done to prospective friends in confidence. It helps to build trust. People tend to consider those who do things for them in confidence more seriously, and are more willing to trust them.

d. Insist on qualitative relationships

It may be difficult to determine the value of a relationship by face value. But a number of factors can point to where the relationship is headed. As mentioned above, people with integrity who are already connected to several other persons make qualitative friends.

e. Follow up on the relationship that you have created

First, maintain a record (online or offline) of your prospective friends. Second, create a system and program to follow them up using physical visits and social media chats. Also watch out for their special occasions and make your presence memorable.

f. Create programs that are likely to solicit their inputs (not necessarily money)

Readiness of others to make inputs to your program is a show of reciprocity and demonstrates a willingness to remain in the relationship. People naturally love to offer input to the programs of those they appreciate or respect. Being ready to offer inputs also indicates a readiness to have a stake.

g. Do not assume that they are too busy or will not help you

Do not hesitate to seek help or support for your program from prospective friends, especially where it may not cost then much. You just have to expect either a yes or no answer. Do not be discourage at the first instance if the answer is no. Asking a prospective friend for support within the sphere of their competence shows that you trust and have faith in their capabilities. Create an opportunity to thank them if they oblige you, and try to reciprocate their kindness.

h. Decide on a visitation/communication plan

Have your personal schedule set for visiting and chatting with your prospective or regular friends and follow it without letting them to know that you actually have a preplanned program.

i. Build networks around yourself

You are better off networking with qualitative friends/partners from different backgrounds, professions, countries, regions, and so on. The network of people will offer you several learning opportunities. Learn from the opportunities while you share your knowledge as much as you can. Position yourself as a unique value contributor.

J. Be likable

Your likability increases with your kindness and being grateful for what you gain from others.

SOURCES

https://ctb.ku.edu/en/help-taking-action

https://www.lifehack.org/articles/communication/5-ways-to-build-stronger-relationships.html

https://www.aspeninstitute.org/blog-posts/reflections-on-building-and-sustaining-relationships/

https://www.dialysistech.net/images/Hale_-_Building__Sustaining_Relationships.pdf

www.ingramcontent.com/pod-product-compliance
Lightning Source LLC
Chambersburg PA
CBHW050309220526
45465CB00005B/1914